ARTIE and BONES

Justin,
Hat Always. Remember
Kindness
Rocks!

Art Direction: Toni Field
Illustration: Toni Field

Field, Toni
  Artie and Bones: a story
of friendship, kindness
and creativity/
 Toni Field;
 illustrated by Toni Field
 32 p.

Artie and his friend Bones
go on adventures to
spread kindness in the
community by painting
rocks to brighten the days
of others.

Freehold, New Jersey

The Story of
ARTIE and BONES
is dedicated to:

PICCINO

I would like to say a special Thank You to my loving husband and son for all their dedication, support and contributions to this project.

I would also like to thank all those people who inspired me to create ARTIE and BONES including my husband and son and the rock painting groups who inspired me to paint rocks for kindness.

A special Thank You goes to my husband Jon, my son Joey, our cousin Jack and our furry family members Piccino, Steeler, Vegas and Miso for inspiring us to create some of the characters in the ARTIE and BONES series.

Heartfelt thanks go to my sweet Piccino. Thank you for inspiring me from Heaven.

The ARTIE and BONES project was created to inspire kindness with the use of art and creativity.

Please visit www.itsaboutart.com/artieandbones to find out how you can share your own stories of kindness.

ARTIE and BONES

A Story of Friendship, Kindness and Creativity

Written and Illustrated
by
Toni Field

Artie is a dog and he is unlike any other.
Artie is a dog who loves to paint!

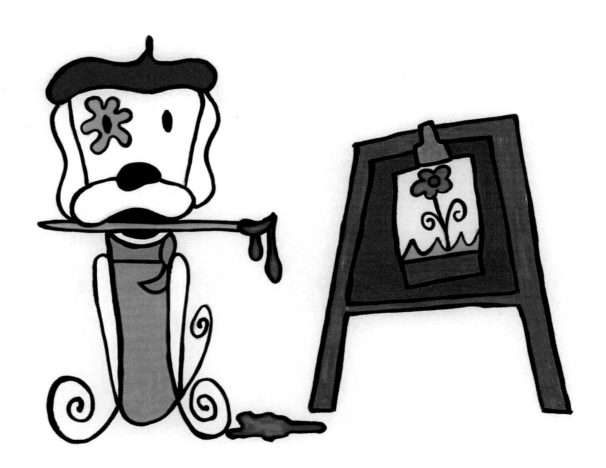

You may wonder how a dog can paint.
For Artie, it's easy, because he has the help
of his friend Bones.

Bones is Artie's "art-ian" angel.
Some people have a guardian angel to
guide them, but Artie has an "art-ian"
angel who inspires his creativity.

Artie is the only one who can see and talk to Bones and that is what makes their relationship so special.

One day, Artie and Bones went for a walk. Artie noticed all the people around the town. Some of them were happy and some were sad. Some were excited and some were mad.

Artie sat and wondered, "Wouldn't it be nice if I painted pictures for the people of the community?"
"I could paint all kinds of pictures for all kinds of people."

Artie wanted to start painting right away,
but all he had was his loaded paint brush.
He didn't have anything to paint on.

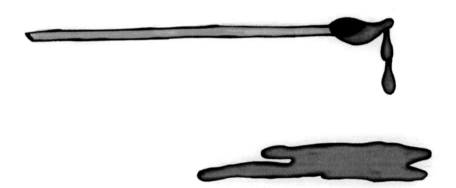

Just then, Bones had a great idea!
He noticed a bunch of rocks lying on the
ground. The rocks didn't belong to
anybody and they would be perfect for
Artie to paint on.

Artie began painting on the rocks. He painted on big rocks and on small rocks. It didn't matter what the shape or size. Artie turned each rock into a beautiful masterpiece.

Artie suddenly had a thought.
"Who will ever believe that I painted these rocks and how will I give them to the people of the community?"

At that moment, Bones came up with a wonderful idea! Since Artie was the only one who could see and talk to Bones, they would use his magical "art-ian" angel powers to deliver the rocks to the people.

And so they did.
Bones started hiding Artie's painted rocks
all over the town with hope that the people
of the community would find them.

The people of the community began
finding the beautifully painted rocks all
over the town.
Whenever someone would find a rock, it
would brighten their day and that of those
around them.

It especially brightened Artie's day
whenever the townspeople found one of
his painted rocks.
It brought him so much joy to know that
he was finally able to share his kind heart
and creative talents with the community.

Artie was so thankful for Bones and all of his help that day. They both realized that they started something very special. They were spreading kindness with their creativity and they couldn't wait to see where this kindness journey would take them.

48504169R00020

Made in the USA
Middletown, DE
21 September 2017